DESIGN STAR

Lessons from the New York School of Flower Design

Half Full Press

DESIGN STAR

Lessons from the New York School of Flower Design

MICHAEL GAFFNEY

Photography by Keith Lewis and Matthew Bushey

Thanks to those in the floral industry who inspired or helped make this book and my career possible. Thanks to Thom and Alex and the Ariston Floral Boutique NYC, Nick and staff at Nuckton Co. of San Francisco, John and George Kantakis and staff at Associated Cut Flower NYC, Rob Bond of Half Full Press in Oakland, and all the students who have attended my schools and with whom I've had the honor to instruct in the art of design. Finally, a thank you to one of my very most favorite retail stores in America, George Watts and Sons, for many of the table settings seen in the book.

This book is inspired by the prettiest flower in my garden — Patricia Gaffney.

DESIGN STAR

Copyright © 2011 by Michael Gaffney
Photography © by Keith Lewis and Matthew Bushey
Edited by Jennifer Harter
Design by Angie Hinh

Published in 2011 by
Half Full Press
1814 Franklin Street, Suite 603
Oakland, CA 94612
(800) 841-0873

10 9 8 7 6 5 4 3 2 1

ISBN 0-9719552-4-7

    978-0-9719552-4-0

Printed and bound in China

contents

I first met Michael Gaffney five years ago while I was putting on a lecture on floral arranging for the Milwaukee Garden Club. Following the lecture, he introduced himself to me and said that he had some rough ideas about also taking advantage of people's love for flower arranging and their desire to "make a splash" with their arrangements. As I had been putting on lectures around the world for fifteen years on this very subject (and knew full well how difficult it is to obtain a following), I politely dismissed his aspirations as naïve pie in the sky.

How colossally wrong I was. I should have bought stock in the man the day I met him. In five short years, Michael has come from relative obscurity to being a major national force in the floral design industry. Hardly a week goes by when I don't see Michael appearing on major television shows (*The Today Show*, *The Morning Show*, *Miami Morning*, etc.) or being featured

foreword

at society events and highly-coveted fashion shows (Macy's Flower Show, Neiman Marcus, Bloomingdale's, etc.).

What is most remarkable, however, is the reality that Michael has extracted some basic design elements from nature, art, and architecture and has created an 8-week course that does in fact convert an enthusiastic wanna-be florist into a full-fledged, operating, profitable, professional florist.

His graduating students not only have hands-on experience from his course, but, more importantly, the personal confidence to stretch well beyond their modest time in the industry. Clearly, Michael has been able to draw on his own many years of experience in the floral industry, provide various step-by-step formulae for the most popular, classic arrangements, and thereby consolidate the key elements into teachable "truths." Through the sheer force of his dynamic personality, insights, and artistic talents, Michael

has taken a cottage industry into the 21st century. To his great credit, he has withheld none of the secrets that most florists guard closely, and instead has freely laid out the secrets to maximizing one's profits, whether as a corner florist or as a floral designer/consultant for weddings and other upscale events. If his graduates have their way, I think we will start to see really beautiful and fully-appreciated arrangements quickly taking the place of the usual lackluster arrangements that are phoned in on the basis of online images (that rarely bear any relation to the finished product).

Not only has he created the New York School of Flower Design course, but he has sold-out schools in Chicago, Los Angeles, San Francisco, and Miami. Who knows where else he will spell his magic? I never thought it would be possible to have twenty-five students in a class and launch them all into a professional career. What is

most praiseworthy is his willingness to share his insights and knowledge with the public through this well-written and wonderfully illustrated how-to book. I have always felt that anyone can create beautiful flower arrangements if they have the tools. Now Michael makes those tools available to anyone who has the interest and the desire to become a professional florist.

In short, I am amazed at the sheer expanse of his many talents — professional flower designer in his own right, architect of national (maybe international when you read this) schools of floral design, knowledgeable and supremely self-confident speaker in front of both the camera and classes and, more importantly, an honest man who has imparted his knowledge to make many others happy and successful. High praise for Michael Gaffney.

Ron Morgan

introduction

Twenty years ago, I was on my way back to Wall Street, with a job waiting for me at a commodities company, when I took a part-time job driving a truck for a flower shop for a couple of extra bucks. A gentleman grabbed me on my way out the door and said, "Wait a minute. Help us with these flowers before you go." And I said, "No way, I don't do flowers." He said, "Today you do. It's easy. Stick a red flower here. It's called a focal point." And I was hooked. I never made it back to Wall Street. I stayed at that flower shop and worked alongside the owner for six years. Every time he did anything, every flower he put into every arrangement, I'd ask him why he was doing it the way he was, and he'd show me. It was halfway between being a Zen Buddhist trainee and an architecture student.

This book will help demystify flower design. It will teach you the rules of design and give you the tricks and tips you need to become a top designer. Flower design is as much architecture as it is art. Think of flowers as color swatches and particular shapes, and when you know the principles of design, when you have the tips and tricks and secret formulae, you'll know exactly where they belong.

It has less to do with artistic ability than you might think. Flower designers are not always creative geniuses who wake up each morning feeling the artistic juices flowing. Can you imagine saying to a bride, "Can you move your wedding to next weekend? I'm just not feeling it today." It is as much architecture as art. I don't ever reinvent the wheel. I do, however, put my own thumb print on my finished work, that finishing touch which makes it unique.

I have schools in seven cities across the country, training people how to become top designers. I do weddings, I do events, I do it all. I have done shows for companies such as Nieman Marcus, Bloomingdale's, and Saks Fifth Avenue. I have been asked to do movies in New York for Natalie Portman, Jennifer Aniston, and Phillip Seymore Hoffman. I have taught employees at Harpo Studios and Martha Stewart Radio. It happened to me; it can happen to you!

design

I have taught many people how to design and have launched many successful careers. Start thinking like a designer right now. Get in the habit of staring at beautiful flowers. One of the first steps to becoming a great designer is to build a database of great design in the back of your head. If you don't know what a gorgeous bridal bouquet looks like, how will you ever be able to create one yourself? Look at other designers' work, in magazines, online, and on TV, and begin to build a library of beautiful images. Those images will manifest from the back of your mind right out of your fingertips.

Flower design is based primarily on what the human eye expects to see. Just follow the lines of nature. The flowers you'll be working with each grow in a particular way. Leather leaf fern has a very definite curve to it, but if you didn't know any better you might stick it into a vase backwards or upside down. It will absolutely look ugly, because it doesn't exist in nature that way.

Putting flowers together in a beautiful way is much like working a Rubik's Cube; it is a formula to be followed more than an artistic creation.

I don't get out of bed each morning and think about the glorious masterpieces I'll create that day. I don't reinvent the wheel when I go to work every day. I build formulaic flower design much like construction. And it can be done when you're not in the mood or half asleep. Practice, practice, practice! Memorize the formulae so that they come naturally; tear your design apart and do it again so that is becomes second nature.

There are two types of arrangements in the world: one-sided, with a definite front side from which it is to be viewed; and all-around, which, much like the name suggests, is intended to be viewed from all sides. So rather than asking yourself what fabulous creation you're going to make, ask yourself: one-sided or all-around? Second question: what style? Classic dozen roses? English urn? French country? American? Every design has its formula, and there are steps to get you to that perfect look each time.

Cross to the left, spin to the right!

Most flower shops will sell loose flowers wrapped up tightly in tissue paper, which always looks a bit underwhelming. They don't look like they're worth the price tag, and they certainly don't look good enough to impress the person for whom they are being bought. This design is perfect for sending flowers to go and will enable you to take any old pile of flowers and make them look gorgeous. It's striking with white Casablanca lilies for a wedding, or with stalks of wheat and berries tied with raffia in the fall.

Pick up a single stem with your left hand. You'll always be designing in your left hand and adding flowers with your right, so your dominant hand is doing all the work. (If you're a lefty, hold in your right hand and add flowers with your left.) Hold the first flower about three-quarters of the way up. Where you hold the flowers will determine where the crown is—too high and it's a tight bridal bouquet; too low and it's a big splayed out mess.

With your right hand, pick up your next flower and add it away from you, at an angle, right on top of your left hand. It should create an "X" with the stems. The flower you just added should be pointing to your left shoulder. Now, place your right hand over your left to grab the bouquet, let go completely with your left, and spin the flowers to the right a full rotation until the flower you just added is pointing to your right shoulder. Just barely lift that left hand off the bouquet and re-grab it at the same height.

Cross to the left, spin to the right. (lefties: cross to the right, spin to the

left). You'll do the exact same move with each stem you add. Add a stem crossed to the left, and crank the whole bouquet to the right. Keep a nice loose grip as you go—if you have a death grip on them, all the heads will end up pointing straight into the air. Don't white knuckle it. Think about having tea with the Queen, holding on lightly with your pointer finger and thumb, and daintily splaying the rest of your fingers out.

Continue adding stems one at a time, spinning after each addition. You want the top of the bouquet to have a nice flat top; if any stems fall deep down in the design or stick too far up, adjust them. You can hold more flowers than you think you can, but towards the end, when you have a full hand, the flowers will hold each other—up to a point. Add all of your flowers and finish your design off by collaring it with a bit of wax flower, crossing to the left and spinning to the right with each addition.

To wire the bouquet, turn it so the top faces the wall and your hand is on top of it. Point the left index finger out, and with your right hand, place two or three wires down on top of where you've been gripping the bouquet. Use your index finger to push the wire around to the underside of the bouquet; turn it upright and pinch the two ends of the wire together with your right hand tight enough that you can let go completely with your left.

Get your left hand underneath the stems and flip the whole bouquet to the right several times. You'll be able to get a tighter tie on it by using the weight of the flowers than you could by twist-tying the wires by hand.

Grab the stems and squeeze them together to give them a nice even cut. Cut them at least as long as the crown of the bouquet, which is the distance from the top of the wire. To finish the bouquet, grip it with your index fingers and thumbs just above the wire (tea with the Queen!), and pound the stems on your table to drive the center stems toward the ceiling. The entire bouquet will splay out and open up beautifully. Keep pounding until the stems are even enough for the bouquet to stand on its own.

classic dozen roses vased

6-5-1 One of the reasons you can never make a dozen roses from the grocery store look good, even after messing around with them for hours, is that you're sticking all of the stems straight down into the vase where they can't really move. Flowers dropped straight down into a vase look rigid and stiff, as if they're connected to the table. There's only so much space in the neck of the vase for the stems to occupy; they have nowhere to go when they're plopped in that way. All of your stems should be landing in the top two thirds of the vase; nothing should be touching the bottom. Perfectly designed roses will look like they're floating and will have a full windshield wiper effect. With this design, we're creating a dome effect with a penthouse, an upper deck, and a lower deck. This formula will give you perfect flowers every time.

Another secret of great looking roses is that grocery stores and flower shops never give you enough greens to properly fill the vase; you'll have three or four stems with the twelve roses. We're going to grid our greens with a star within a star pattern, and "clogging the drain" in the vase with them.

Take the first piece of leather leaf fern, remove most of the stem, and angle it across the vase with some of the leaves down the drain. Take the second piece, cut off some stem, and overlap it across the first. Turn the vase each time you add a stem. Repeat with a third, fourth, fifth, and sixth piece of fern. You should hear a "crunching" sound each time you add greenery—it may sound bad, but it's good! That rustling means the greens

are creating a nice tight grid that will hold your flowers in place. When you're done, you should have a lovely six-pointed star. This is your lower deck, resting on the rim of the vase.

Next, for the star within a star, cut a little less stem off and place a piece of fern just shy of straight up in the air, or the penthouse, down into the upper deck. Turn your vase, and overlap a second, third, and fourth piece of fern, rotating the vase as you go. You should have a four-pointed star sitting atop the original six-pointed star.

For the penthouse, take two pieces of fern and face them together, as if they're kissing, leaving most of the stem on so they're nice and tall and will rest above the four-pointed star in the upper deck. Right down the middle goes "the kiss," jammed into the rest of your greens. It ought to be pretty already even without the flowers, like a fresh green plant growing out of a vase. Now you've gridded your greens and the flowers will hold in place wherever you put them (much better than dropping everything into a vase, letting go, and hoping for the best!).

The formula for a dozen roses in a vase is: 6-5-1. Six roses in the lower deck, five roses in the upper deck, and one rose in the penthouse.

Find your tightest, most closed rose of the bunch and set it aside for the penthouse. That perfect bud will help tell the story of the roses as they grow, small and tight, and reaching for the sun.

For your lower deck, the stems

should be cut to one and a half times the height of the vase. The secret to a perfect vase of roses? The lower deck goes in underneath the greens, not on top of them. Hold each stem way down low, like a writing pen, for maximum control, and feed them in across the vase. Place six roses around the vase, going under the greens rather than within them. Rotate the vase as you go, so the stems are evenly spaced. Imagine setting a piece of glass down on top of them when you're done—if you've done it right, and they're all the same height and evenly spaced, you should have a little coffee table. Tweak any stems that are too long or too short to bring them all to the

same level.

The upper deck gets placed way up top, just shy of straight up in the penthouse, but slightly off center. You want a definite distinction between levels, like tiers on a wedding cake, or it will look like a crowded mess. Cut your upper deck roses so they're two times the height of your vase. Again, holding them way down low, feed all five in evenly.

"Run up the flag" with the tight bud you set aside for the penthouse. The stem length should also be twice the height of the vase. You should have a full windshield wiper effect—a nice round dome of gorgeous roses.

A lot of florists would send this out just as it is, but the aim of this book is to teach you how to be top designers. Accordingly, we're going to take it a step further and re-green and add filler. That pretty star within a star we created is lost, and there are naked stems, making the whole design look a little empty and lacking.

To re-green, start with a collar of fern all around the lower deck. You may not need another complete six-pointed star, but go all the way around the vase and add what you need to give the design a support system. These are called the "footlights" of a design, and they visually hold up the entire arrangement. Add a few pieces

The client isn't buying a vase of greens; they're buying a vase of roses. Now it ought to look nice and full, like a cut rose bush sitting in a vase.

Texturing your greens is another way to add visual interest to a design; great designers will use several different greens to give their work more texture. Add some nicer greens, such as pittosporum or seeded eucalyptus, perhaps some bear grass shooting out, the same way you re-greened.

Repeat the formula for filler: six in the lower deck, five in the upper deck, and one good piece in the penthouse to keep the top rose company.

6-5-1 will give you a perfect dozen roses every time. For two dozen, or even three or four dozen if the guy at the counter has done something really horrible, just double up the numbers or add more layers. This also works well with any number of flowers: a dozen irises, gerbera daisies, or tulips.

of fern to the upper deck to hide the naked stems, and two stems straight up in the penthouse, making sure not to cover up any of the roses. You don't want the greens to overpower. They should come up to the head of the rose but never hide any of it.

"The B&B" Unlike American design, which is evenly spaced and a bit more sprawling, classic English design is tight and short. The European style of flower arranging is about styling flowers, head to head, with little or no greenery.

Our greens, in fact, aren't even going to show in this design—they're purely mechanical to clog the drain of the vase and hold our flowers in place. To build a star within a star in your hands, start backwards with the kiss, two stems facing each other.

Then, add a piece of greenery to the left and spin the whole thing to the right. Much like a spiral staircase, keep adding a step and turning it. When you have a nice handful, or a "carrot top," slide your hand up the greens so you're holding a tuft, which is all you need. Cut the stems down short, and clean off the rest of the leaves below your hand so they don't muck up the water. Jam the carrot top down into the neck of the vase. It doesn't have to be particularly pretty—once the flowers are in place it will completely disappear.

There are two basic types of flowers in the world: line flowers and mass flowers. Line flowers are long and slender, like snapdragons, delphinium, and gladiolas. Mass flowers are full and round, like lilies, roses, and daisies. This is a mass design. Use full, open blooms in English design; you won't find many tiny closed buds in an arrangement such as this. The more open and large your flowers are, the quicker it will go, too.

The focal point will be right at the top of the arrangement and will act like fireworks—BOOM! A big, strong

center to draw the client in, then trailing out so they can take in the rest of the design as well. Take three roses and group them together for the focal point. The height of English design is equal to or less than the height of the vase. Measure your vase with your hand and place the three roses at roughly the same height.

Now fill in the igloo. Each flower you add is another block of ice. Imagine a metronome on a piano—tick, tick—it will swing a full 180 degrees. Want to know where your next flower should go? Hold it up next to the penthouse and swing it down along the same angle like a metronome. Follow that line. Your stems should be landing in the widest part of the vase, and not any deeper. If they hit the bottom of the vase they'll point straight up, even though you've set them in at an angle. We want a nice round snow globe.

After you've set your penthouse with your primary flower as a focal point, set your lower deck. It's much easier to design in that order, because you can simply fill in between the penthouse and lower deck. Keep the vase turning as you work, and add flowers into your upper deck, nestled up against the penthouse, then back down to your lower deck.

If any of your greenery is poking out, trim it down. If any greenery is used in English design, it will be added at the end, collared around the lower deck.

This is a very labor-intensive design, so it's expensive. It isn't the type of arrangement you'd want to do in a busy shop on a Monday morning when you're way behind. (turn to page 100 for tropical design for a nice quick arrangement—bird of paradise, orchid, anthurium, a couple of leaves, and out the door!) You'll see tight English looks like this at the Grammy Awards and at high-end weddings—giant globes of flowers in different height towers all over the place, for around $3,000 a table.

I call this the "B&B"; it should be at every bedside table in every bed and breakfast. If you pulled it out of the vase and ran off to City Hall to elope, you'd have yourself a little bridal bouquet. All it's missing is a ribbon. Get back to the room, plop it back into the vase, and no one would be the wiser!

all rose hand-tied bouquet

"The Martha" The all rose hand-tied bouquet is the number one most requested bridal bouquet in America. You've seen it, you've loved it, and the secret is, it couldn't be any easier. You can put one together in about ninety seconds flat. Sure, you'll spend fifteen minutes fussing with it to get it just right, but it really is the easiest bouquet in the world to do.

This is called a hand-tied bouquet, meaning the stems are left on and wrapped in ribbon. (As opposed to cascade bouquets, which are fairly out of fashion, and all the stems have to be either individually wired or stuck into one of those foam holders with the plastic handles. Whenever a bride tells me she wants a cascade bouquet, I wrinkle my nose and say, "Really? I used to do those a lot in the 80s..." and she'll change her mind.)

Start with nice, big, open roses. Tight "bullet" looking roses won't stay in place the same way. Your very first rose is Sting in concert. "Roxanne!" Hold him way up high. Now add the VIP seats in the front row, all surrounding Sting. Cross each rose to the left, laying it down almost totally sideways and then pulling it in so it sits underneath Sting. Turn the whole bouquet to the right after each rose you add. The VIP

seats are Larry (cross to the left, pull it in close, spin to the right) and his date Sally (cross to the left, pull it in, spin to the right) then Bob and his buddy Fred and their dates Suzy and Mary. The first row should be between five and six roses to surround Sting, depending on how big they are. If you were to stop here, collar with a little pitt and tie it with ribbon, and you'd have a flower girl bouquet.

Theater seats will be set up so they're between the seats in front of them, so you're not staring at the back of somebody's head. For the second row of the Sting concert, the roses will sit right in between the roses of the first row. Add your roses with your right hand, always away from you so you can look down your nose at the bouquet and make sure it stays nice and rounded. You want to almost lose sight of each row when you look down at that dome of flowers. Keep

it nice and rounded—you don't want a pancake-shaped bouquet! Keep your eye on Sting after every few additions, and pull him up a bit if you need to. He should always be the highest point in the bouquet—he's headlining.

Second row seats are added the same way. Tweak as needed, pulling up any roses that have fallen down, or pulling down any that are sticking too far up. If you were to stop here, you'd have a bridesmaid bouquet. Repeat with a third row. Rose bridal bouquets will be between eighteen and twenty-four roses, depending on how big the roses are.

The human eye expects to see a little greenery with flowers, without

which the bouquet would look a bit naked. Collar the bouquet with a few stems of greenery, pittosporum, or even hypericum berries, adding them just as you did the rows of roses.

Pull them way down low, making sure they're just barely peeking out beneath that last row of roses, not competing with them.

Wire the bouquet by holding it sideways, roses facing the wall, dropping a couple of wires down right where you've been holding the stems, and using your pointer finger to push them to the other side. Once you have both ends of the wire together, pinch them together tightly, let go with your left hand so you're just holding onto the wires in your right, and twirl the whole bouquet a few times to tighten the wire. Hold all the stems together to get a nice even cut on them, clean any stray leaves or thorns off, and pop it into a vase of water filled all the way to the top so the greens hit the water.

On the morning of the wedding, pull the bouquet out of the vase and lay it down on a couple of paper towels to dry. Either clip the ends of the wires off, or, if you're lazy or in a hurry, stick them up into the bouquet to hide them.

I have seen many, many brides carrying a giant baseball bat of a bouquet, lugging a tree trunk down the aisle. The stems are four or five inches around. The trick to keeping it looking light and lovely: cut the "junk out of the trunk." Get in under the "hoop skirt" of the outer stems and cut out about half the stems from the inside. The bouquet won't be in water from this point on, so don't worry about those roses dying faster than the rest. Now you have a nice, chic, manageable bouquet.

To smooth out some of the bumps in the stems, wrap them tightly in 1" floral tape before you ribbon wrap. To wrap the bouquet stems in ribbon, take a length of double-faced

satin ribbon about a yard long, and start at the top, right where your wire held it all together. There's no need to pin it here—just tighten with your right hand as you turn the handle of the bouquet in your left; that will be enough to hold it into place. Pull it tight as you go, and wrap it all the way to the bottom. To secure the ribbon, insert pearl head pins in and up through the bouquet stems at an angle, like administering an IV, not straight through. It looks particularly nice lined all the way up the stems when the bride has matching buttons on her gown.

Other great looks beyond the wedding day: picture a few of these in cubes down your dining table, or in the entryway of your house. I've seen these at every elevator bank at a casino opening, up in big tall cylinder vases with trailing ribbon. Couldn't be any easier!

"The Michael" When I first started out in this business, I spent a lot of time and energy being nervous about whether my bridal bouquets would turn out. Why did last week's look gorgeous and this week's fall flat? And then I really sat down and analyzed what made last week's so much prettier, and a pattern emerged. The bouquets that were only so-so were more random in terms of flower placement, and the really drop-dead gorgeous ones that hit you right between the eyes had geometric shapes.

Organize your flowers like a poker hand, starting with the prettiest and working your way down to filler and greenery. For a bouquet of Casablanca lilies, roses, stock, freesia, wax flower, and pittosporum, you would place them in that order. You don't have to necessarily know a lot about flowers to know that the lilies are the star of the show, and that the roses are nicer than

the stock, which is bigger and more impressive looking than the freesia. Use your most premium flower as a focal point, and then work your way out in geometric shapes.

Cluster the lilies in the center as a focal point and then surround them with roses—let's say a square of roses. Crossing to the left and spinning to the right, add four roses around your lilies. Then continue to go down the poker hand. Add a pentagon of stock, five stems. Perhaps a hexagon of freesia. If the bride really loves roses, and many of them do, you can go back and add another shape of roses, let's say a pentagon. Collar with wax flower and greens in the same way, spacing them evenly and putting them into a deliberate shape.

Placing your flowers in triangles of three, squares of four, pentagons of five, or hexagons of six around a central focal point works every time. It makes a collection of flowers visible all at once. Nice, symmetrical patterns are easier to take in—don't make the bride work on her wedding day, looking at her bouquet and looking at it some more trying to decide if she likes it or not. Show her great design. The patterned mixed bouquets are very graphic and gorgeous. I call them "The Michael," as opposed to a bouquet composed entirely of one type of flower, which I call "The Martha."

hydrangea bouquet

The hydrangea-based bouquet is all over the magazines—it's all the rage. It's a very classic bridal look, and the good news is that it's a very easy look to create. Hydrangeas will act as a flower holder for every other flower you add to them.

Start with two or three stems for a bridal bouquet, depending on how large the flower heads are. Clean the leaves off; otherwise, they'll get damaged when you start threading flowers through them. Put the hydrangeas together so they make as rounded a shape as possible; if it's a little lopsided in certain spots you can trim it down like a hedge. Holding the stems high up will help keep the bouquet in shape.

Now you have a flower holder. Strip roses and tulips nice and clean so they don't do any damage to the hydrangeas. Thread them into the hydrangeas so they nestle just inside the blooms. Don't neglect symmetry—create geometric shapes just like the mixed bridal bouquet. If you have four tulips, put them in a square; if you have half a dozen roses, either a hexagon or two triangles. Finish it off with a collar of pittosporum or some hypericum berries, wire and ribbon wrap, and you've got a gorgeous bridal bouquet that's one of the hottest looks around.

This is also a very pretty look for centerpieces; picture several of them in little cubes running down a long dining table, or a cylinder topping each table at a wedding to coordinate with the bridal bouquets. And the great news is they're nearly effortless to make.

A lot of florists are afraid to work with hydrangeas because they have a tendency to collapse. They'll look perfect, then all of a sudden on the way to the church, they wilt and look like a wet rag. Here are the secrets to making your hydrangeas last: first, as soon as you get them home from the market, soak them upside down in a bucket of water for half an hour. Hydrangeas can drink through their petals, and keeping them as hydrated as possible will help them live longer. Second, dip the cut stems in alum, a product used in canning and preserving that you can find in high-end grocery stores. Hydrangea stems are thick and woody, so water doesn't travel up them very easily. Alum opens the stems up and forces them to take a nice long drink. Lastly, spray them down with a

product called Crowning Glory, which is essentially a wax coating for cut flowers. It will help seal in the moisture and keep them looking nice and perky.

wiring and taping

The ability to tape and wire flowers for boutonnières, corsages, and head wreaths makes you very, **very** employable for wedding work. When interviewing for a job, the first words out of your lips ought to be, "I know how to tape and wire." (As opposed to what most people say, which is, "Well, people say I'm very creative, and I really love flowers." Not at all what a shop owner is looking for. Would you apply to an architecture firm and tell them you really love buildings?) Not everyone enjoys taping and wiring—it can be tedious work. So those rare employees who love it (and some do!) get sent to the back room to crank out all of the boutonnières and corsages for all the weddings lined up each weekend, and I don't see them until they're finished.

When wiring flowers, what you're doing is essentially replacing the natural stem with a wire stem. Cut the stem of the flower down so there's just enough to hold onto, 1/4" to 1/2". Using a half length of wire, about 6" or so, pierce the calyx of the flower, the small ball at the base. Run the wire through the stem and then gently fold it down in half.

If the stem of the flower isn't thick enough for the pierce method (mums, for example, have a very slender little stem), you'll use the insertion method. Leave just enough stem to hold onto, run a length of wire parallel to the stem, and stick the end up into the underside of the bloom. Some florists use a hook method, where they hook the end of the wire back down into the head of the flower, but it's more damaging and time-consuming, and isn't really necessary.

To wire foliage, stitch the wire through the back of the leaf way down low. Go over the center vein, and back out the back of the leaf, like you're sewing. Run it through gently, fold it in half, and you have a wearable leaf. Silk leaves are available at floral supply stores; they have wire built in and are

ready to go. Some high-end florists won't use them, but I've definitely been guilty when I have several weddings on the books and need to save some time. Students often ask if rose leaves can be wired and taped and used in boutonnières and corsages, and the answer is NO, they won't hold up long enough to make it through an event.

At some point in your career, you'll need one more rose for a boutonnière, and all you'll have left is a snapped off head lying on the floor that doesn't have enough stem to hold onto. If you were to wire it without any stem for the tape to grip, the flower head would fall forward on the lapel, and one groomsman will have a hanging rose in all of the wedding photographs. Instead of running out and buying another bunch of 25 roses for the one boutonnière, you can salvage the broken one from the floor by cross wiring it. Pierce one wire, then take a second and pierce it through perpendicularly, so you have an "X." Fold both sets of wires down, and the rose is as good as new.

To tape your flowers, take a roll of 1/2" floral tape and start wrapping it around at the very base of the flower where the wire begins. Spin the flower with your left hand and pull the tape tight with your right as you go. The secret to fast taping is that we aren't going to roll it all the way down. Once you have it started, give the tape a good pull straight down the

wire, and it will cover it up. Most of the bottom of the wire is getting trimmed off anyhow, so it doesn't need to be perfect. This move will save you a lot of time!

The average retail price for a boutonnière will be around $10. Could be a little less for a smaller one —$7.50 or so; could be a bit more for premium flowers—$12.50; but figure on an average of 10 bucks. It may only be a dollar's worth of flowers, but the cost will be $10. The markup is high because there's so much labor involved. The average corsage will sell for $25 to $30, with about $5 or $6 worth of flowers being used.

Boutonnières are generally three flowers or less; any more than that and you're in corsage territory. Boutonnières are one-sided designs. You'll be designing between your fingertips. Wire and tape all the elements you plan on including.

Start with a focal flower, such as a rose, and add a leaf behind it as a backing. The secret to quick and light boutonnières is banding. When they catch and tag a bird, they put a little ID band around its ankle. That's all the tape you need to use each time you add another element; just a 1/2" band at the very top. Band it with a bit of tape. Now, cut the "junk out of the trunk"—cut off all the wire from the leaf you just added, right below the band of tape, leaving just the wires from the focal flower. Each time you add another element, band it in, then cut the "junk out of the trunk."

Filler and berries can be added without taping and wiring them first, since they have such thin woody stems.

Once you have all your elements in place, add a leaf at the very base of the boutonnière, cupping the bottom of your focal flower to cover up your mechanics and support your design. You should only have the original wires from the first flower left, so it shouldn't be a giant tree trunk. Give the whole thing a final taping, this time all the way to the bottom. Some florists will use a pen or pencil to wrap the wires around and make a cute little curlicue, although I prefer a straight stem. I think the curly tail is visually interesting, but I can't keep a good grip on them and I end up dropping boutonnières left and right, usually with a line of five guys waiting for me to pin them, and I'm looking over my shoulder to make sure the bride isn't seeing me trashing her flowers.

Boutonnières get fastened to the left side of the jacket, over the heart. No one told me that when I started out in this business. I figured since most people are right-handed, flowers ought to go on the right side, but I guessed wrong (oops!). Most people pin boutonnières too low, and they look lazy in the photographs. Pin them up nice and high so they look fresh.

Trim down all of the flowers, leaves, and filler you plan to use; then wire and tape everything. Speed is so incredibly important in this business, and taking the time to snip one flower at a time, put down your clippers, pick up your wire, pick up your tape, and then do it again six more times for a single corsage is not the speedy way to do it. You'll hardly ever be making just one corsage or boutonnière—you may need to make a dozen for a wedding, or maybe there are 60 orders for a prom. This book is training you to be a top design professional and a valuable employee; your boss will be watching to see how quickly you work. If you have everything wired and taped, and, better yet, laid out in order ready to go, you will absolutely impress.

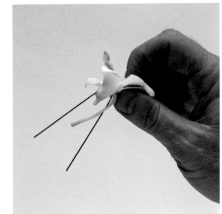

In the old days, corsages used to be monstrous 12- or 15- flower deals. The giant ones are out of fashion these days; most corsages will be between five and seven flowers total. For a seven-flower corsage, start with the tightest closed bud—to tell the story of the flower growing. Add a leaf behind it, band it with a piece of tape, and cut the wires from the leaf out right under the band so only the original bud wires are left. You'll be working left to right, moving down in your design every time you add a flower. Each flower you add will be slightly larger than the one

before, so the weight of the design is at the bottom. When it's done, it ought to be shaped like a Christmas tree.

Add your second flower, slightly larger than the bud, right on top rather than behind, to build depth into the design. Set it off at an angle, making sure it's not choked too close to the initial "tree trunk" of the first wire. You want to be able to wriggle it and reposition it to exactly where you want it. That's why you replace the original flower stem with wire, so you have the ability to manipulate it. When you've got it positioned, band it, and cut the "junk out of the trunk."

Your third flower goes off to the right, lower than the last. Once you get the hang of it, you can add a couple of elements at a time—put a piece of filler or another leaf in with your flower. Band it all together, and cut out all the junk.

Flowers four and five should be your largest focal flowers. Add number four off to the left, with another leaf, band it, cut the junk out. Add number five to the right, with filler or a leaf as needed, band it, and cut the junk. If you need to cover up some wires, you can add filler in between the flowers to hide those mechanics.

The final two flowers should be slightly smaller than the last, to lighten up the design so it isn't an exact triangle (which is bottom-heavy). Add a couple of leaves cupped underneath the final flowers to support the design. If you lose track of which was your original wire from the first flower, or if you run out of that wire, you can switch to another. After you've banded in the last element and cut the last of the "junk out of the trunk," give the whole thing a final taping all the way down. Adjust so that all your flowers and leaves are nice and even and right where you want them.

I always do a few seconds of adjustments when I pin on a corsage or slip one on a wrist, even if it doesn't need it. I'll pretend, and they just eat it up. Little insider's secret.

Head wreaths are built in much the same way as boutonnières and corsages, but with a few key differences. For a flower girl, you'll need about twenty-five to thirty flowers, which will give you a length of about 22". (Don't ask me why, but every little girl's head is 22" around. If you really want to measure, you can take a length of ribbon and wrap it around her head and that's your length.)

Start by wiring all of the flowers you'll be using, then banding them with a bit of tape. Instead of staggering the flowers left to right like a corsage, add one directly underneath the other. If you branch out too far left or right, you'll end up with a very thick head wreath. Stack the flowers on top of each other, and tape them together. Leave the "junk in the trunk"—the extra wire will add weight and structure to the wreath. Remember, just like boutonnières and corsages, this is a one-sided design. The flower girl's head goes on the inside! When you come to the end (and this will take a while— usually around forty-five minutes), loop the end of the last taped wire around the first flower to secure it. If you're adding trailing ribbon, it would go over the intersection point.

Wreaths can be as different as the style of the wedding. They can be thick and English for a formal ceremony. They can be skinny little

hippie wreaths for barefoot beach weddings. You can make wreaths in patterns, like wallpaper.

Again, wire work is very labor-intensive, which means it's also very expensive. Head wreaths start at about $50 for a simplistic one of daisies and a lot of baby's breath to fill in the gaps. Most head wreaths, however, will run around $150. If you think about it, a head wreath is essentially a bunch of corsages all the way around a head—if a single corsage is $25, why wouldn't a bunch of them together be $150? Most brides are happy to spend it, and money is no object when it comes to the flower girl. However, if you're on a strict budget, there is a cheater version: you can create a wreath shape out of heather or ivy by winding wire around the strands, and add just a few stems of flowers in with glue. It isn't as pretty, but it works in a pinch.

vertical line design

Vertical line design is the "Monday morning quarterback" of the flower shop—quick and simple, a big "scopey" look for less money than other larger pieces. It's a one-sided design incorporating a lot of negative space, so there are fewer flowers, but has a big impact. Also, it's considered a contemporary look, so it breaks the rules of height in classic American design and is much taller.

Start by foaming in your container: cut soaked floral foam down to size and push it gently but firmly down into the container. If there are empty spaces down the sides, block them in with smaller slices. Leave about an inch of foam above the rim of the container, so stems can be inserted horizontally into the lower deck. Think about a green plant from the nursery, how some leaves grow up, and others grow out. Bad design will all be coming up from the container, with nothing coming out horizontally, so the arrangement looks like it's sinking in quicksand.

Begin with your line flowers, because that's what the human eye expects to see in nature—flowers

growing, reaching for the sky. Line flowers serve to draw the eye from the outer edges of a design down deeper, where the mass flowers can be the focal point, and they give the eye a place to rest.

Work from the back of the foam to the front, placing flowers from left to right. You don't need to insert them really deep, no more than an inch or so. If you go "drilling for oil," you run into trouble with your foam breaking up. Use the entire foam, as opposed to jamming all of the stems right into the center. Novice designers don't use up the foam they have—be sure to work it.

Two stems of liatris, one shorter than the first, then two stems of snapdragons. Work your way down the mountain of your arrangement. Don't be afraid to make large cuts to your stems—you want to bring the color all the way down from the top of your tallest flower to the rim of your container. Your container is a part of the design, too. If everything is way up in the air, there's nowhere for the eye to rest, and the look is chaotic.

Once you're toward the bottom third of the arrangement, switch to mass flowers (in this case, Asiatic lilies and roses) and start to angle them so they face the audience. That slight tilt will make all the difference in the design, giving it a focal point that's easy to see and take in.

To finish it off, we're going to utilize some contemporary greening. With minimal greens, you get a more modern, sleek look. A few stems of pittisporum, terrace, or stack, some galax leaves, and fill in with sheet moss soaked in water to bring it back to life. To hold your moss in place, snip down wire so it's a few inches long and bend it into a hairpin shape to create a staple.

Another great technique to incorporate in this design is framing—take a couple stems of curly willow branches and insert them on the outside of the arrangement, so they're pointing in at your flowers. This tells the human eye, "Hey, look over here! Isn't this gorgeous?" It makes a big impact for just a couple of sticks added at the end.

This is a nice tall arrangement that's only a few stems of flowers. The clean, vertical lines make it very showy for as few materials as you're using. You'll see this look in every online delivery service, in coffee mugs, or baskets and the like. It will get you though much of your delivery work; when someone has $40 or so to spend on Grandma's "Get Well Soon" at the hospital, but it still needs to make an impact—and make Grandma's day.

basing

This is the hottest look in centerpieces—it's in all the hotels, restaurants, and all over the magazines. It's a simple, clean look, drawing a tall vertical line and creating a dome of mass flowers as a base below.

Foam in your container, leaving enough over the rim to insert flowers horizontally. Start with your vertical element. Good materials to use include dogwood, forsythia, pussy willow, or curly willow. Set the branches right in the center of the foam.

Now we simply base at the bottom. Start with your lower deck, cutting the stems nice and short so the flower heads hit just beyond the rim of the container. Insert the lower deck flowers horizontally, to create that nice rounded dome shape. Cluster a few stems up around your branches as a penthouse, then simply fill in the upper deck between them.

61

It's a gorgeous look for weddings if the bride wants to go up in the air, but doesn't have the budget for the tall glassware rental. It's perfect in groups of three or four down a dining table for a dinner party. You'll spot it in store front window displays like crazy, in fashionable little cube vases. And now you can make it—it's a quick and easy design.

parallel design

If you were to come into my house, you'd find parallel design everywhere—I have sharp, parallel systems in cubes all over the place; down the tables, in the bathroom, you name it. They're contemporary, urban, masculine looks; cool and clean.

Start with a full block of foam, and work left to right. Create a line of flowers coming from the back of your foam to the front of your foam, staggering down in height. Think of the New York skyline—start with your Empire State Building. In front of that, staggered off slightly to the left or right, is the Chrysler Building. The third building is a thirty-story apartment complex on the street, and the fourth and fifth are little retail stores, maybe a flower shop, and a sidewalk cafe. Now you have a system of parallel flowers.

Move over to the right in your foam, and create another parallel system with a different type of flower. You don't need to smash the systems

right up alongside each other—space them out, give them plenty of breathing room. This design utilizes a lot of negative space, meaning that much of the impact and interest is in the empty air space where there aren't any flowers. Less is more in clean, modern design such as this. Don't be afraid to make money on empty air space!

In this design, we have parallel systems out of liatris, snapdragons, some stock, and roses. Almost any flower, line or mass, will work in a parallel system. You can also add

systems horizontally, so they look like they're running through the arrangement.

Each system should have a very dramatic drop in color, from the tip top of the highest building all the way down to the sidewalk. It should take your eye from the top to the bottom very quickly, almost like an elevator falling. You'll be making big cuts on your stems—if your first building is a hundred stories, your next stem should be at least a third to a half shorter than the one before it.

Finish it off with minimalist greening to match the rest of the design. Terrace a few galax leaves and cover up your foam with pitt and

moss. Although you don't have to necessarily create parallel systems out of your greenery, be sure to group your like materials together so the look is cohesive. Frame the design in with some stems of bear grass or branches.

Parallel design is a great opportunity to look on the floor and utilize some material that would otherwise get swept up and thrown in the garbage—create a system or two out of your cut stems and sticks. Something that would otherwise have been wasted is now a valuable product that you charge your customer money. That's great design!

wreath

Back in the days before floral foam wreath forms became available, wreaths were based on either straw or river cane and flowers were all glued in. The foam forms make them much easier, although they're still quite labor intensive. You'll find them in funeral work, at weddings, and on church doors and garden gates to mark the ceremony spot. And, of course, they're ever so popular come the holidays, with evergreens and berries.

Two variations of wreaths are scatter and pattern. A scatter wreath is made exactly the way it sounds—by scattering all of your flowers throughout the wreath. Make sure to band all around, meaning to cover both the inside band and the outside band and not just the top of the foam.

Trim the stems of your flowers nice and short, no more than 1/2", because you don't want to go "drilling for oil" with them. If they're too long, your flowers will either stick out the other side of your foam, where they'll have no water and die, or they'll run into each other in the foam, making you reposition them and leaving you

with Swiss cheese for foam. Once the flowers start to drink water, the foam will condense and hold onto your stems even tighter, so don't feel they need to be deep down in there to stay in place.

Scatter wreaths are particularly nice in all greens, perhaps succulents and moss, or with just a few blooms of flowers used throughout. They don't have to be all flowers to make an impact.

A clock pattern wreath creates focal points and works out from the primary flowers in your poker hand down to the greens and moss. Start with your focal flower and place either one or a cluster of several at 12:00, 3:00, 6:00, and 9:00 on the top of your wreath, as if it were the face of a clock. Then, surround each focal flower with the next nicest flower in your poker hand, making sure to curve around the outer and inner edges.

Repeat the pattern with your third flower, around the bull's-eye you've got in place. If you've run out of room to circle completely, band on either side of the second flowers. Leave enough space in between each insertion so the flowers have a bit of breathing room—you don't want it looking like a packed subway car, and you don't want to be using more flowers than you have to.

Continue down the line of your poker hand, finishing off with fresh greenery, such as galax leaves and pitt, and a touch of moss here and there, which will give the wreath an organic, fresh look.

pave

Pave is a French jeweler's term, which comes from the word "pavement." Think diamond wedding bands and cobblestone streets. It's a very modern, contemporary look.

I like my pave designs to look like corn fields, as if you're looking down rows of nice straight flowers. I call it the Warhol approach to flower design—repetition and pattern. Although you could do more of a Monet in pave—swirls of flowers. There are different approaches. I've sent cigar boxes filled with pave bark, roses, and stones, all tied up like a box of chocolates.

Drive your flowers straight down into the foam, creating whatever pattern you choose. Surround the edges of the design with moss, or pitt and galax leaves. You can frame the whole thing in neatly with lengths of bamboo or river cane for a nice, finished look. You can even run a few pieces of sticks through the design to separate the rows like you're farming. There are a lot of directions you can go with a look this clean and modern—pave never fails to impress!

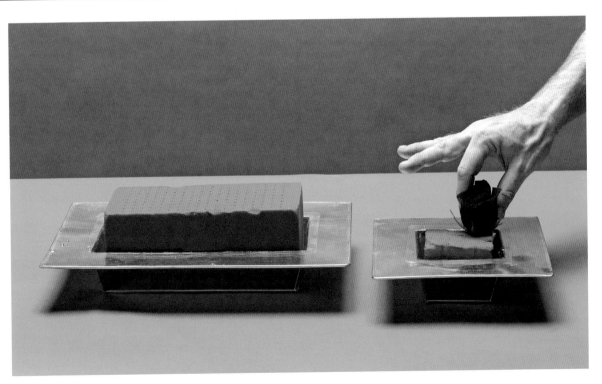

ball topiary

To create a ball topiary, soak a foam ball in water and drive it onto a river cane pole. Use a thick band of floral tape to create a stopper a few inches from the top so the ball doesn't come sliding down like New Year's Eve in Times Square. Remember, this design will be top-heavy. Choose a weighty glass container to foam in for the base, otherwise you risk the entire creation toppling over. You can always weigh it down with rocks if needed. The taller you go with your pole, the more likely it will be to wobble. You'll be fighting gravity with this design. Like any design with this many flowers individually inserted, it's time consuming, so if something goes wrong, you'll need plenty of time for repairs.

Once your foam sphere is in place, use mass flowers and simply

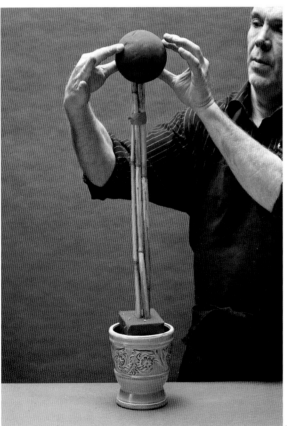

pave in the whole ball. Finish the base off with some simple greens and moss, and perhaps a few stems of flowers from the top to carry the color down and bring unity to the design.

You'll see similar spheres of flowers with satin ribbons at weddings, either on shepherd's hooks lining the aisle, or as pomanders for the flower girl to carry.

To create a pomander, as opposed to a topiary, simply run a few pieces of wire through the center of your soaked sphere, with a looped end to string the ribbon through. If your flower girl is going to be rambunctious, or if there are two flower girls (which are more than twice as hyper as one), you may want to finish the pomander off with floral glue to make sure it holds up for the photos.

lily topiary

"The 4 Minute Topiary" This is a look I have my delivery drivers do on busy weekends. They look at me like I'm crazy, but they can put them together and have them out the door in no time flat. I certainly don't ever tell my brides that. "Yes, my drivers Fred and Jim will be doing your wedding flowers." Not something I share with the client. But it really is a foolproof enough design that anybody can do it and it will be a knockout.

Tear all the leaves off your lilies so you have nice clean stems. Take a length of river cane or bamboo pole to run up the center for stability. Lily stems can bend, and we want them nice and straight. Arrange a full bunch of lilies around the pole, keeping your stems very straight. If some of your blooms are more open than others, place them toward the outer edge of the design. Create as uniform and round a shape as you can. Don't worry if most of your blooms aren't open yet—as they start to open they'll push each other down, and gravity will help give you more of a ball shape.

When you have it all in place, secure it together with a length of wire or with floral tape. You can hide the mechanics later with moss, ribbon, or the like. Holding the bottom stems together, drive the whole thing straight

down into the center of your foam. Decorate the base with whatever blooms have broken off, with moss and a little greenery.

This is a great look for brides who want to go up in the air for their table centerpieces, but can't afford the $300 price tag for that type of glassware. It's tall and impressive without overwhelming the table. You can still see across the way clearly. I've sold this centerpiece over and over again, using giant white Casablanca lilies with stems of bear grass shooting out from the topiary.

Roses, peonies, and hydrangeas work well for this design. Sunflowers for an outdoor country wedding would be lovely. You can dress the topiary up or down depending on the container and the greenery you choose—baskets versus mirrored glass cubes, a bow of raffia versus ivy trailing down the stems. It's a diverse look, and it couldn't be any easier to put together. My drivers could crank out about forty of these in an hour.

mixed vased

When you're interviewing at a flower shop and they ask you to do an arrangement for them, this is the one to do. The mixed vased arrangement represents the majority of all orders sold in a shop. When a customer calls or comes in, they'll be asked if they want their flowers wrapped or in a vase. Most will choose a vase, thereby precluding making the recipient mess with them when they get the flowers home. This design will enable you to take any old pile of flowers and make them into a beautiful design, in twenty minutes or less. Once you know this formula, you should be able to know without really looking hard where every flower ought to go. You can walk into the cooler, grab a few stems of this, a few stems of that, and it will turn out looking good every single time.

To start, green in your vase with the star within a star. Work backwards in your hand, beginning with the kiss, then crossing to the left and turning to the right until you have a decent cluster of greens. Trim them down into a carrot top, clean off the leaves that will hit the water, and stick them into the vase. Most of these initial greens are going to  disappear once flowers get added, so don't spend forever trying to make them look pretty. Once the carrot top is in place, add greens on your lower deck, going in across the neck of the vase, upper deck, at about a forty-five-degree angle, and penthouse, straight up in the air. You'll be re-greening after your flowers are all in, so it doesn't need to be perfect—it's mostly mechanical.

Here's the simple formula: start with the queen in your poker hand, your showiest flower. Place those in the upper

deck as your focal point. In mixed design, the focal point is in the upper deck, right there at eye level facing the audience. If you have three stems, put them in a triangle in the upper deck; if you have four, put a square, and so on.

Put your line flowers in the penthouse, at the very top of your design. The maximum height of classic American design such as this is three times the height of the vase. Set your height with your line flowers, which will draw the eye down into the rest of the design.

Go down your poker hand, adding more premium flowers to the upper deck, where they can be seen better. The lesser flowers are down in your lower deck. Be sure to go across the vase for your lower deck, so the stems are flared out at a nice angle to give you the full windshield wiper effect. If everything is sticking straight up, the design looks choked rather than full. Turn the vase as you work, so that you're placing flowers evenly and symmetrically. Use geometric shapes, putting in triangles, squares, and pentagons.

Make sure not to bury any of your flowers underneath greens or other flowers—think of a snow globe. All of your color should be on the top of that dome, not hidden in it.

Your flowers should be resting on top of your greens. Novices will stick the flowers deep down in the greens, and they will get lost in the jungle.

Go all the way down your poker hand, getting flowers into all of your decks and the spaces in between. Last, but not least, comes the filler, which will cover up many imperfections. Think of the filler as the mortar between the bricks—it holds the whole thing together. Add the filler into the penthouse, the upper deck, and the lower deck.

Now re-green, going back and getting greens into the lower deck across the vase, the upper deck, and the penthouse. Be careful not to cover up any of your flowers. Greens ought to nestle just below the heads, to support, but not overpower. You can use more premium greenery than you did for the initial mechanical greens, such as pitt or seeded eucalyptus, to add texture.

This is a classic American design, the number one seller in flower shops. It works for grandmas, it works for coworkers, it works for lovers. It's a good look for entertaining. Now you'll know what to do when you buy loose flowers from the farmers' market or someone brings you an ugly mixed bouquet from the grocery store.

triangle design

All floral designs are either one-sided or viewed all around. Triangular design is a one-sided design. It's the foundation for a great deal of bridal, corporate, and funeral work. It's very radial—think of a sunburst in a triangle shape. To create this shape, we are going to build a "man."

The first piece of greenery forms the body and sets the height of the design. In classic American design, the container is one-third the height of the finished piece.

Next, we add the legs, which are smaller than the body. They determine the width of the piece. The body is set in the back of the foam, and the legs up at the front, giving depth to the design.

Next, the arms go in between to

complete the triangle shape. Lastly, we add footlights at the front, giving support to the design.

This is formula designing, as we will repeat these steps again using smaller body, legs, arms, and footlights. Flowers follow the greening—we place the flowers in the same pattern.

classic candle centerpiece

This is a classic oblong centerpiece that's a popular look for the holidays, usually placed in the middle of the dining table with the fancy tablecloth and Grandma's china. It's a good look for the head table at weddings as well.

Start with a full block of foam, and set your taper candles in place, down the center, in plastic adapters. Make sure they're nice and secure—the tablecloth and Grandma's hair are flammable, and you don't want to ruin Thanksgiving with a fire. If you're using large pieces of fruit, or any other non-floral mechanic besides the candles, set them into place now, before the greens. Otherwise, you'll have to move greenery out of the way to make room, which is a waste of greens, and things are more likely to be unstable if the greens are in the way.

Once your candles are in place, begin greening. With greenery, start with your least attractive greens first, since they'll be covered by flowers and not as visible. Work your way up to the prettier greenery to texture after your flowers are in place.

Build in a penthouse, an upper deck, and a lower deck, nice and close to the foam. This isn't a very tall design—people need to be able to see across the table and ask someone to pass the gravy. Keep your greens close to the foam. The lower deck defines the perimeter around the piece, and the penthouse defines the height. Be sure to include some legs on the sides of your foam, mirroring the oblong shape of it. Add a few pieces right at the corners and edges of the block of foam to round out the brick shape. When you're done,

you want it to look like a green leafy armadillo.

Don't worry about having some spots of foam visible—your flowers will take up a lot of real estate and cover up most of the empty holes. It's better to under-green than over-green, which is the tendency of most novice designers. Every piece of material you put into your design costs you time and money. And, if you have too many greens at the beginning, you run out of space for your flowers. Remember, you'll be coming back and re-greening after your flowers are in place, so you can always hide holes if you still have them.

Flowering follows greening—your flowers get set in right on top of the dome of the greens you have in place. Start with a focal flower in your upper deck, facing the audience

at the dining table. If you have three big gerbera daisies, place them in a triangle around your candles. Keep your mass flowers toward the center of the design to serve as focal points, and add your line flowers into the side of the foam, with the greenery "legs" to give the design movement. I call this the lava approach, almost as if the arrangement is erupting down the center of the table.

Get your lower deck nice and low, close to the very base of your foam. Think about the kids sitting at the table and try to make sure they have flowers to look at down their level, too. Just like you did with your greens, place some flowers at the corners and edges of the foam to round it out—you want a radial form, not one that is clunky or brick-like.

This is a very radial design—imagine all of the flowers shooting out from an imaginary point in the middle of the foam. Finish it off with a filler and a second or third type of green. It's a great "cooler cleaner" arrangement to make, because you can throw just about any flower into it and have it look good. Everything but the kitchen sink. And you are now indispensable at Thanksgiving and Christmas—once your family gets wind that you can make this centerpiece, you'll be expected to show up with one at every holiday.

tropical

Tropical design incorporates negative and positive space. The flowers, which are big and showy, are your positive space, and in tropical design, a little goes a long way. All the empty air space between the flowers is negative space. You're making money on something that isn't there, which is always nice.

The most common flowers used in tropical design are orchids, birds of paradise, heliconia, ginger, anthurium, and ti leaves. You can certainly use flowers that aren't actually tropical—pincushion protea, for example—as long as it fits with the general "jungle" look of the design.

Tropical flowers are stored at room temperature, not in the cooler. They'll freeze in the fridge. Think cool Hawaiian nights, not cold New York mornings.

Start from the back of your foam and work your way forward. Add your flowers staggered from left to right. In tropical design, unlike contemporary work, you want all of your flowers to look as if they're growing from one plant. Everything should be coming from an imaginary central point of growth, so no parallel "goal post" looking lines, and no crossed stems. Flowers don't grow in nature that way.

Set your height with your tallest stems, and work them left to right, bringing the color down as you go. Don't be afraid to cut down quite a bit of those stems. Your design can be symmetrical or asymmetrical. Make sure not to bury any flowers under bigger blooms.

Every piece of greenery counts in this type of design. Use minimal greens. Terrace a few galax leaves above some moss. Stems of bear grass shooting out from the base will add nice movement without competing with the flowers.

When I run out of ideas, I often run to Home Depot and roam the aisles until I find something interesting, like copper tubing from the plumbing department. Who says you need to send $100 worth of flowers to impress a new client? Here is a simple, ten-minute design using just four flowers, a bit of greenery, and some unexpected materials. This "companion piece" design cost approximately $10 wholesale for both pieces!

Wire the gerbera daisies to support their stems. Insert a wire through the head of the flower parallel to the stem, then wind the wire around it. To line the containers with ti leaves, shave down the thick membrane on the back of each leaf so it becomes more pliable, and then work it around the foam in each container, like you're wallpapering the inside of the vase.

A few lengths of river cane, loops of copper tubing and decorative wire, and minimal greens complete the design. I've used very little material; this is a chance to show off your creative side. Find unusual materials and create architectural, artsy looks. When flowers and metals are combined, it's always a real attention-getter. It can be the perfect look for an art gallery opening, a man's office, or a new restaurant. Great design for less.

gallery

Every design tells a story.

114

The best flower designs disappear in a few weeks. Floral design is a very ethereal form of art in that way.

To be a designer, you have to live, think, and move like a designer.

I love my brides and I do everything to make them the star.

I've opened many doors with a beautiful bouquet in my hands leading the way.

124

Many of our students have been featured in national publications, and we have launched many great careers!

Great design brings great joy.

Great design is like a beautifully designed billboard—it stops you in your tracks.

Flowers can soften the hardest personality.

We teach
saleable,
commercial
design.

140

Florists are in the business of making people happy and celebrating important milestones in life.

Cross to the left,
turn to the right!

I've never had a student who did not create great works of floral design.

Just do it! Buy it! Design it! Collect the money and go home happy.

Living and working as a designer is a privilege.

153

There's no such thing as a Bridezilla—it's a myth.

"A good artist borrows from other artists; a great artist steals."

—Picasso

Make the
design
look like it
was born
that way; it
doesn't need
any more or
any less.

163

Floral design is easy. If you're struggling, you're doing something wrong.

Flower design is based primarily on
what the human eye expects to see.

There's a method to the madness that enables our students to create great flower designs.

I call it the
science
of beauty.
Years ago,
I figured out
the patterns
and formulae
of great
design.

Stare at beautiful images of flowers, and
we will teach you the rest. One day it
will just flow out of your fingertips.

The best designers are always willing to share their knowledge.

Flowers are seen at all occasions—from birth to death.

You always beat the client's expectations; after all, this is what you do for a living.

You're the next design star!

profit

There is money to be made in flowers. Every weekend there are $500,000 events happening across the country. Yes, we are in a recession, but couples are still getting married. They may be more frugal than they would have been a decade ago, but weddings occur nonetheless. And there is still money to be made on smaller weddings; a $3,000 wedding will have a cost of goods of about $1,000, leaving a profit of $2,000. And that would be for three or four days of work. Keep in mind that flowers are perishable, so it isn't as if you will be working on each event for weeks on end. If you have a $30,000 wedding, you would be making $20,000 for a four-day week. I know artists who set up 300 canvases for a weekend street festival, sell a few of them, and have to haul all the rest back to their studios where they pile up for years, collecting dust. And they remain emotionally attached to each of them. The temporary nature of flowers is one of my favorite aspects of this business—you do the design, you get paid, it goes out the door, and it disappears in two weeks.

There is more to the business of flower design than design. I know plenty of top designers who are unemployed right now, simply because they can only design, and they don't have a good grasp of business. The business aspect is the other side of design—you have to be a good salesperson as well as a good designer, and it takes about as much practice to get it right. The single easiest and most effective way to market yourself is to get your business card out into the world. Start networking like crazy; tell everyone you come across that you're a floral designer. Hand your business card out at every available opportunity—give one to your hairdresser, the bus boy, the cab driver.

I rank my students in my head from 1 to 10. My 10's are the ones I can't believe have never designed before—they pick up flowers for the first time and it looks as if they've been doing it for years. My 4's (and 4 is about as low as I'll rank) have less of the raw talent, but have always proven to be the most successful in business. One of my graduates from the Chicago School of Flower Design was from Brazil, and admitted at the end of the course that she hadn't

199

picked up half of what I said in class. She's now running a hugely successful event company in Brazil, designing like a pro. When she first started out, she kept her designs very simple, like big vases of grasses down long buffet tables, before developing her own unique style. Another one of my 4's from the Milwaukee School of Flower Design used to be an MBA and decided she wanted a career change. She walked into my classroom and said, "I'm going to be a floral designer. This is what I'm going to do." And she held steady at a 4 and she never really mastered any design. But the week after she graduated, she went to an art gallery opening with a really basic, easy-to-do arrangement of curly willow branches with stems of dendrobium orchids rung around the neck of the vase, and a big stack of business cards. $26 worth of flowers singlehandedly launched her new career. She's so busy now, she has assistants that do most of her designing for her, and she's been featured in *The Bride and Bloom* magazine twice. I can't even get in that magazine!

Many of the looks these days are simple to do. It's a wonderful time to be a designer, as opposed to the 80s when all we did were enormous Dutch masterpieces. The high-style looks are clean and simple, and you learn to put your thumb print on them to make them your own. My favorite florist in New York is Ariston, which has locations on Chelsea and Lexington. It's a hugely successful family business specializing in events and weddings. They can do it all, but they basically sell these gorgeous all-mass designs of hydrangeas, ranunculus, and peonies, in cubes and cylinders, over and over again. Simple, salable, and they do them very well. They are a huge extended family of men from Greece. I tell them I used to be a truck driver, and they say, "Our forefathers were sheepherders."

The two things that kill flowers are bacteria in the water and surface evaporation. To combat water loss from the surface, dunk your flowers head first into a

"Many of the looks these days are simple to do. It's a wonderful time to be a designer, as opposed to the 80s when all we did were enormous Dutch masterpieces."

bucket of water as soon as you get them home, and let them soak for a good half hour. They'll last twice as long. I once did a destination wedding in the Bahamas, where I brought in $3,000 worth of orchids, but was delayed at the airport. I ended up at the nearest hotel, with all my wilting orchids in the bathtub covered in every towel in the room to keep them from floating to the top. I got about thirty minutes of sleep, packed the orchids back up, and took them back to catch the next flight. Some kid at the airport said, "Hey mister, your box is leaking." The flowers were perfect for the wedding, but they never would have survived without that bath.

For years, you've probably been putting that powdered stuff in vases to kill bacteria in the water, which actually deteriorates the straw and makes it more difficult for the flower to drink.

And if your flowers come with two packets, you've probably figured, "Well, if one is good, two is even better," and sprinkled both of them in there. Honestly, they do more harm than good. Because it's a solid dissolved into a liquid, the powders are meant to be put in the water twenty-four hours before the flowers touch it, but of course no one ever takes that kind of time. Think about sugar in iced tea—you end up with chunks of solid particles floating around in there. All the powder does is clog your stems. Adding a little bleach to your water will kill bacteria and keep your flowers alive longer.

Elaine Matashta, the editor of the *Chicago Tribune Garden Section*, called me once and asked the one

thing I couldn't go without professionally, and my answer was Crowning Glory. It's a floral product that's essentially a wax sealant that laminates your flowers. I told her I've never had a wilted flower in twenty-three years, and Crowning Glory is the miracle product that makes it possible. I sent her a bottle and she put it on the front page of the *Tribune Garden Section*.

Half of the job of a floral designer is designing—the other half is sales. If you don't know how to effectively sell a bride, it doesn't matter how talented a designer you are, because you won't book anything. You need to fine-tune your selling technique, and find a script that works for you—you'll say the same things over and over to brides that walk through your door. It takes knowledge, confidence, and the ability to put a bride's mind at ease. Basically, she wants to know she's going to be in good hands for her wedding. Let her know you're the one for the job as soon as you speak with her. And for the record, there is no such thing as a Bridezilla. They're all sweet, lovely, and happy to be getting married. I've had a few tense brides, but never any who were unpleasant to work with. It's a television myth.

Sell a wedding in three parts: personal flowers, which are the ones carried down the aisle; ceremony, which is everything at the ceremony site; and, lastly, the reception, which is everything at the party. That way, you can break up the price quotes into three parts as well, and tell her $800 for going down the aisle, $2,000 for the ceremony, and $4,500 for the reception. I'll keep reiterating these figures as we talk so she doesn't go away thinking she heard the whole wedding would cost $800. It's a nice sensible way to break the wedding costs into chunks.

When a bride walks into your shop, give her a verbal resume. "Hi, congratulations on your upcoming wedding. My name is Michael Gaffney, I'm the director of the New York School of Flower Design. I have schools all across the country, in Chicago, Milwaukee, Minneapolis, San Francisco, San Diego, and Los Angeles. I've been doing weddings for twenty-three years. I've worked for companies such as Nieman Marcus, Bloomingdale's, Saks 5th Avenue; I've done film work for Phillip Seymore Hoffman and Natalie Portman. My next door neighbor loves my work; I've been doing her flowers for years. And my prices are very competitive for top-quality flowers. I've never had a wilted flower in twenty-three years, because I have access to the best product in the world. And I don't charge a servicing fee or labor, which most other florists do. If you have a $200 bouquet, you're carrying $200 worth of flowers down the aisle. I'll take care of everything on your wedding day; you won't have to worry about a thing, just glide through the day with gorgeous flowers. I'm really looking forward to designing your

wedding. Let's talk about your day."

I tell her right up front I'll be doing her wedding; I make it easy for her to book me. Already, before we've even talked flowers, she's thinking, "Why would I go anywhere else? Best flowers, best prices; he's giving me something for free without me asking..."

When I say, "Tell me about your wedding," most brides will say roughly the same thing. "It's very formal," or "It's fairly casual." They all say, "My dress is really different," and "I love roses," or "I love hydrangeas."

I'll ask about the dress first, because you can design the entire wedding from the bride's bouquet. And usually, when she's going on and on about what her dress looks like, I'm wondering, "Hmm, I wonder what my horses are doing down at the barn right now..." I'm not a gown designer. Basically, I want to know if she's going to be wearing a big Oscar de la Renta ball gown, or a slim Calvin Klein sheath, so I can coordinate her bouquet accordingly.

Think of the dress as the gallery wall, and the bouquet as the artwork.

For a full ball gown, or an ornate dress covered in beading, I'll slim down the bouquet so it doesn't get lost in the chaos. For a simple sheath, I tend to make the flowers slightly busier.

Then I'll ask what color the bridesmaids are wearing. Let's say it's sea foam green for an early summer wedding. I'll look into her eyes and tell her, "You know what I love for a summer wedding in pale green? For you, green hydrangeas, since you love hydrangeas, and white Casablanca lilies, which have that to-die-for fragrance and look so good amongst hydrangeas. I love white stock nestled in, and a scattering of white roses to really make it a wedding. I love green hypericum berries, because berries lend it that summer feel. Do you like a touch of lavender? Maybe a little hint of lavender wax flower, and a collar of variegated pittosporum leaves. For the bridesmaids, I love all of the above, minus the Casablanca lilies—we'll save those for your bouquet."

I give her a description of what I think she should carry, and half the brides nod through the entire talk, even though I'm sure they don't know

"I take my time describing flowers to her...I want to be able to paint a vivid picture for her. I'm selling her a vision."

what most of the flowers are that I'm suggesting. 99% of brides want you to guide them through this process. Most of them don't have the first clue about flowers. You're the expert, and they're relying on you to guide the sale. Occasionally, a bride will come in with some very specific ideas in mind—she has a binder bursting at the seams with magazine clippings—but more often than not, what she's picked out won't work. It's either wrong for her wedding, or she can't afford it, and you'll end up redesigning from the ground up anyhow.

"For the groom and groomsmen, let's do a little white dendrobium orchid on the lapel—very James Bond." I say that to everyone, about every boutonnière, so she goes home and says, "Oh honey, you'll love it, he's going to make you look like James Bond!" "For the mothers and grandmothers," I continue, "Let's send them down the aisle with little hand-tied bouquets rather than corsages—it's the latest trend." So now I'm telling her about the current styles. "Instead of a wristlet or a pin-on, they can hold a collection of flowers they can later set down at their table. Makes them look like a bridesmaid, takes twenty years off them, they love it! How does that all sound?"

I take my time describing flowers to her; keeping in mind she may not know what any of them look like at all, so I want to be able to paint a vivid picture for her. I'm selling her a vision. We haven't opened up a flower book at this point, and I rarely do. She'll flip through for ages and lose the pages she liked—just confusing things. Keep it simple. I let her know we're just brainstorming at this point, and that she doesn't have to make any concrete decisions today.

And then I'll ask if she wants to know the average cost of a wedding like the one I'm describing. For the bridal bouquet, you're looking at between $150-$200. Bridesmaid bouquets average $65-$85. And this is for top-quality, drop-dead gorgeous flowers—just keep driving that point home. Boutonnières are around $10 to $15 depending on the type of flowers we use. Hand-tied bouquets for the mothers start at around $40, whereas corsages are $18-$25. And then I'll ballpark the bridal party cost for her, and I'll always go on the high end of what I quoted. For a wedding with five bridesmaids, I'll do five times $85, plus $200 for the bride, and I usually tack on an additional $200 for the remaining boutonnières and such. I'll tell her, "You're looking at about $800 to go down the aisle, for all of the personal flowers."

Then I'll focus on the ceremony. I'll ask her, "Are you concerned about the ceremony?" Sometimes she'll say no, she's got it all set. It's a really gorgeous church that doesn't need much, or her mother-in-law is planning on decorating, or what have you. And I'll still give her some ideas to think about. "What I really like at a church wedding are big urns going down the aisle, like the entrance to Rome, with branches so you're walking down under a canopy." She might say she loves it, but it sounds expensive, and will ask what it would cost. I'll quote her about $3,000, and if she says, "No, no, my fiancé will kill me," then I come down in scope from there. "Alright, I also love the look of flower boxes coming down the aisle, sort of a modern garden take on rose petals." At that point she might say

her mother-in-law wants to stick bows on all the pews; I'll try and steer her toward a fresh flower option. I'll even go so far as to wrinkle my nose at ideas I hate. "You know, no one's really doing the bow thing anymore. And for not much more than you'd be spending on ribbon, I can do a bit of fresh greenery on each pew, with some seeded eucalyptus and some long arching strands of bear grass, so you still get that runway effect. We can do every 3rd or 4th pew for about $400." I'll put some options in her mind, and about half of them come back wanting the biggest look we talked about.

Finally, the reception. I'll ask, "Are you concerned about the reception?" And if she shakes her head and says no, I ask her what's going on the tables, and usually the mother-in-law is up to something, or the site has some big ugly hurricane vases with pillar candles they can use. The same tactic gets used here; I'll make a few suggestions of things I can do instead.

When you're first starting out in this business, you'll have three or four large centerpieces in your arsenal, three or four medium options, and three or four smaller ones at the ready; she will pick one of these looks. A handful of centerpieces will take you a very long way, and you

> "Keep gorgeous flowers in front of you to build that database in your head. Tear pictures out of magazines, mark pages in books, stare at them on a regular basis."

can make alterations to them. Keep gorgeous flowers in front of you to build that database in your head. Tear pictures out of magazines, mark pages in books, stare at them on a regular basis. Study the looks, and sell what you know you're comfortable doing.

When a bride walks in the door, she's either in the market for a Honda or a Bentley, and you never know which it will be. Early on in my career, I was selling the small weddings, because I was raised in a very middle-class world and couldn't really imagine that anybody would want to spend that much on anything. I didn't know how to sell a Bentley, so I was only offering a Honda. I had a bride leave my shop when I quoted her $3,000, and she went down the street to a competitor who booked her for $22,000. Learn how to sell the Bentley!

Start big and work your way down if you need to. For every bride who walks through my door, I suggest the big, up-in-the-air looks before I mention anything smaller. "You know what I love on tables?" I say, "I love big tall cylinders up in the air, with mounds of green hydrangeas and sprays of white dendrobium orchids shooting out. Then on the table at the base, squares of hydrangeas, lit up from beneath with these fabulous underwater lights, so the whole table has a soft glow. We can scatter green cymbidium orchids all over the tables, just do a nice thick carpet of them, and guests can play with them while they're waiting for their dinner, and tuck them behind their ears. To tie it all together, I love the look of stems of orchids hung on the back of the chairs."

I'm watching the bride as I'm talking to feel her out; she'll either look like she's warming up with each idea I give her, or she's about to have a heart attack. And every bride says the same thing at this point: "I love it, but how much will that cost?" I'll let her know that the look I'm describing will run about $650 per table. At that point, she's either on board and you've sold the Bentley, or you have to pick her up off the floor and come down from there.

If she needs to go lower, I can suggest bringing the centerpieces down to the table. "How about we do some gorgeous silver revere bowls with big mounds of the green hydrangeas, and maybe get playful with the placement

of flowers, and do a little zoning. We could do a zone of white stock, and a zone of those fragrant white Casablanca lilies from your bouquet, and a zone of mixed lavender flowers for a pop of color, with strands of bear grass flying out to all the place settings for a fun summer feel. That would be around $185 a table." I start with the expensive looks, and work my way down until she's comfortable.

She'll either be nodding or shaking her head at this point. If she's

shaking it, "No, no, my fiancé will kill me," we keep coming down. If she loved the silver bowls, I can suggest mint julep cups with mounds of green hydrangea, with tiny matching julep cups placed on each table setting, for $75 a table. And then if she's nodding, I know I'm in a price range she can handle. And many times, brides will come back to me after they've gone for the less expensive option, wanting to bump it up to one of the bigger looks. Once it's in their head, they may not be able to get it out again.

At this point, I'll start to wrap up the meeting by running through what we've discussed again, and ballpark her total. Brides always ask when they ought to let me know by, and in the early years of my career, I would say, "Oh, six to nine months in advance," and they'd feel like they had plenty of time to go shop around. They'd go to work and be talking wedding flowers and a coworker would say, "Oh, my sister-in-law does flowers, she could give you a better price than that I bet, you should call her!" I lost the sale and the bride got crappy flowers from an amateur. So now I convey a sense of urgency. "I'm very busy; I do a lot of weddings, so when you're ready, I'm ready. It's a $200 deposit to book the wedding, and once you book me I'm all yours. You own me till the day of the wedding. If you see something spectacular in a magazine and you want to change everything, you call me and we'll change it all. And I'll be there all day on your wedding day to make sure it's perfect." I make her feel so well taken care of that she doesn't need to talk to anybody else. I've been giving the exact same speech for years, and more often than not, they whip out the checkbook and pay the deposit on the spot.

90% of the time they don't call or come back in to make any alterations. If I don't hear from them a month before the wedding, I call them up to go over everything, and then another quick phone call a week prior to finalize the numbers (four bridesmaids, four groomsmen, two ushers, etc.). Payment in full is due ten days before the wedding, because that's when I'll be placing the orders for flowers.

I had a bride walk into my shop in tears. She'd been turned away from another florist, who wouldn't talk to her for less than $50 a table, when she could only afford $25. On top of that, she was in love with a sleek Calvin Klein gown, but her mother wanted her to wear a traditional Japanese dress, and she was just heartbroken. I handed her a box of tissues and said, "First of all, you'll be walking down the aisle in the Calvin. And second of all, my table centerpieces start at $25. My job is to make your wedding look like a million bucks no matter what your budget is. So dry those eyes." I gave her a single bud vase with one stem of white dendrobium orchids and bear grass arching out across the table. Her bridesmaid dresses were copper, so I went to Home Depot and bought copper wire from the plumbing department, wrapped pieces of bamboo in copper wire and one little orchid head and put them at each place setting. I got polished river rocks from the dollar

Your goal is to create a fantastic vision for your bride. The end result will beat all her expectations!

store and tossed them across the table, amongst little tea lights. It was gorgeous. And more importantly, the bride was thrilled; I had single-handedly made her wedding. I probably booked $40,000 worth of weddings directly off of that wedding, because word-of-mouth is such a powerful marketing tool. She told everyone she knew that I was her hero.

Practice your sales technique. You'll end up with a speech that you'll repeat over and over again. Work on describing flowers in detail; make them sound good enough to eat. Your goal is to sell the bride on a look without her ever setting eyes on it. Without a decent vocabulary and a strong, confident speaking voice, you won't be able to.

People often worry that it will take them forever to learn all the flowers they need to know, but the truth is, there are only a handful that you'll use in wedding work:

Calla Lilies

Freesia

Hydrangeas

Hypericum Berries

Lilies

Orchids

Peonies

Ranunculus

Roses

Stock

Tulips

Throw in a few assorted greens and filler, and that's basically every wedding you'll come across in your career (a couple of very classic bridal flowers that didn't make my list are stephanotis and gardenias, which I avoid because they brown so quickly). Learn to describe these flowers in different combinations and colors, and to describe them well, and you'll be all set. Make sure you sound like you know what you're talking about—if you stammer, "Umm, well, how 'bout some lilies or something? Umm, umm..." that doesn't evoke much confidence. And you can certainly sell the same exact look over and over again. I know a very successful florist in Chicago who has blatantly been doing the same wedding—same bouquets, same boutonnières, same alter piece, same centerpieces—for years. Needless to say, the florist was always busy. Again, sell what you're confident doing. Confidence will land

you the sale.

A few more tidbits of advice: look the part of a designer—I know florists who meet their brides in sweats and clogs, and it always shocks me when they get any business at all. Dress to impress. Throw in something for free. Offer free boutonnières or free delivery. Every bride, no matter what her budget, wants to get something for nothing. Most brides just want to get another thing crossed off their list when it comes to their wedding. Planning a wedding is a lot of work, and you can see the relief in their eyes when they book you and they know they can stop worrying about the flowers (now all they have to worry about is the cake, and the DJ, and the food, and the linens, and the lighting, and the million other things they have to deal with!).

Weddings can be stressful for the florist as well, so keep on top of the details, and make sure to have some help. Take a big sheet of brown paper, write the entire wedding in marker, and tape it up to the wall where you can see it. "JOHNSON WEDDING—SATURDAY, JUNE 12. BRIDE—WHITE CASABLANCA LILIES, WHITE ROSES, WHITE STOCK, LAVENDER WAXFLOWER, GREEN, HYPERICUM, PITT." Otherwise, you're relying on little sheets of paper that get lost in the shuffle, and no one can remember what's in the boutonnières or how many bridesmaids there are. By the end of the weekend, you'll have the details of the wedding memorized, and you'll never have to stop what you're doing to dig around for a lost list.

Have a couple of "warm bodies" around to help. Even if they don't end up helping with flowers, it's good to have someone nearby to tell you if the centerpiece looks good or not, or to run out and grab you a soda. Usually by the end of the weekend, they'll have contributed something in the way of flowers, but even just an extra set of eyes to reassure you that everything isn't ugly is wildly helpful when you're first starting out. They'll keep you calm as they stand around in case you need them. Sisters, friends, and neighbors work well.

I always do my weddings on Wednesdays. Flowers get shipped in on Mondays and Wednesdays. If you wait any later to buy them, flowers that have been cut the

"Sell what you're confident doing. That confidence will land you the sale."

weekend before are sitting around in warehouses, or on trucks, or at the wholesaler being picked over by other florists, just gathering bacteria and dehydrating. Experienced florists don't wait till Saturday morning to do their weddings, or even Friday, because if something goes wrong at that point, you're out of time to fix it. But I rarely have things go wrong, because I have great product from wholesalers whom I know and trust. So I buy my product on Wednesday morning, design bouquets and centerpieces on Wednesday, boutonnières and corsages on Thursday, and have all day Friday to look at that page up on the wall and see if I've forgotten anything.

My record was seven weddings in one weekend. I had the brown paper sheets all over the shop, each with color coded stickers on them to delineate which designers were doing which wedding. Yellow dots were Bobby's, blue dots were Susan's. I had seven weddings, and by Saturday I knew all of them by heart. We did $68,000 that weekend. Each designer took a schlepper, or helper, to haul and unload. Immediately following, I remained eerily calm. At 1:45 in the afternoon on Saturday, I was watering my garden. I'm not a very good gardener, and there isn't much in my garden to water, but I had the hose out, just hoping the phone wouldn't ring with a panicked call about

missing boutonnières or the like. I knew my last bride was walking down the aisle at 2:00. And when 2:00 hit, I knew everything had gone smoothly, turned off the hose, and went home to celebrate.

Find out from the event coordinator what time you're able to install the day of the wedding. Typically, it's about an hour and a half or two hours prior to the ceremony. Start with the flowers for the bride and bridal party, which I have an assistant assigned to do so I don't have to chase people around for an hour. I'll have them all boxed and labeled, and my schelpper can hunt down the last of the three aunts, who's running around pinching kids' cheeks and not holding still long enough to get a corsage pinned on her.

As far as transporting flowers goes, you can buy big expensive boxes and trays specifically designed for flowers, but no one really sees them. I'll have them all unpacked and on the tables before the bride shows up, so I've never bothered to spend the money on them. Your flowers will come in nice, long, sturdy boxes, wrapped in newspaper and tissue paper, and that ought to be all you need to pack everything up. Crumble newspaper up around your vases to cushion the centerpieces, and bouquets can be stood up nice and straight with a cushion of paper so they don't roll around in the back

of the car. And I've never owned a van in all my years as a florist. You can do most weddings in just a small SUV. If your schlepper has an SUV as well, all the better. Jennifer, the designer who teaches the San Francisco School of Flower Design, did her first four years of weddings in a two-door sports car. If you have a bigger event, go to Home Depot and rent a van for $19.99, which is substantially cheaper than paying insurance all year on a huge van that you won't fill to capacity except on rare occasions.

Traditional markup for flowers is three times the wholesale cost. If you buy a rose for $1 wholesale, you sell it for $3. That's the retail price. The typical markup on weddings is three times the wholesale cost of goods, plus a labor charge of between 15-30%. Your labor charge is entirely up to you. If you had a $3,000 wedding, and charged 25% in labor, you'd immediately cut out $750 and pay yourself $750, plus the tripling of your flowers and materials.

You're buying wholesale and selling retail, and the conversion should always be in your head.

Every business-savvy dressmaker and grocer and the like are thinking about wholesale costs and retail costs all the time in order to stay on top of how much money they're making.

If you buy a bunch of twenty-five roses for $25 wholesale, you mark them up three times your cost, and turn around and sell them for $75. If a bunch of stock cost you $7.50, the retail price is $22.50. For an $8 bunch of tulips, which is ten stems, they would be .80 per stem wholesale, and would retail for $2.40. Always be tripling in your head. For a $10,000 wedding, I know my cost of goods will be a third of the total retail price, so around $3,333.33. That includes not only flowers, but foam, wire, vases, pins, ribbon, etc. If I charged the bride $300 for her bouquet, I'll be spending $100 on it, and the rest is profit. "How much is the wax flower today?" And the guy says it's $7.50, which means I have to turn around and sell it for $22.50. I may ask if he can come down a little from there so I'm making the money I want to be making. Prices will fluctuate seasonally. For example, roses are more expensive in February because the demand is so high for Valentine's Day. There is some room to negotiate with your wholesalers. Build a solid relationship and you'll find yourself well taken care of. Bring them a bottle of wine every once in a while to show them you appreciate all they do for you.

To calculate your labor correctly, take the total wholesale cost of goods and divide it by the percentage left over after you subtract your labor.

"There is nothing better for business than a happy bride!"

For that $100, and a 20% labor fee, divide the retail price by .80.

For a $10,000 wedding with a 20% labor charge, subtract 20% of the total retail cost to cover labor and see what you have left to spend on goods. 20% of $10,000 is $2,000, leaving $8,000 retail for the cost of materials. Divide that by three to see what you'll be spending wholesale, which is your total cost of goods. $8,000/3 is $2,666.66—that's what it's costing you to purchase everything you need for the wedding. The remaining $7,333.34 is your profit.

The labor that you charge is entirely up to you. The typical range is between 15-25%, and you can fluctuate according to what you're making. For a smaller arrangement, you can charge less than you would for a larger one. For my bridal work, I don't tend to charge labor at all on the bouquets, because by the time you've subtracted out the chunk to cover labor, you aren't left with much to spend on flowers, and I like my bridal bouquets to look nice and plump. They're the stars of the wedding and I'd rather make a little less money on them than have them looking skimpy. You don't ever want the bride staring at hers between photos thinking, "Hmm, it doesn't look like it should have cost $250..." You want her gazing at it with total bliss and joy. When you're first starting out in your career, I recommend charging little or nothing for labor—you'll book more events, you'll sleep better at night, and you'll still make plenty of money.

Servicing fees are often charged, for delivery, installation, breakdown at the end of the event, pinning on boutonnières and corsages, etc. Those will usually be $40 or $50 a person, or about $500 for the day. Again, it's up to you to decide what you want to charge for servicing. I'll throw it in for many of my weddings, especially if I can see on the bride's face that she's already spending more than she wanted to when she books me. And I'm happy to do it to make the bride happy; although, come midnight, when I'm taking apart an arch and loading it into the car, I'm usually grumbling that I could have been making an extra few hundred bucks. Take good care of the bride, so at the end of the day she's thrilled with her flowers, and thrilled with you. It's worth the freebies you throw in for her. A big part of your job as a designer is to make the bride's day, and it's very, very good for business. She'll tell her friends, who will tell their friends, and you'll stay busy all the time. There is nothing better for business than a happy bride!

bloom

Picasso said, "A good artist borrows from another artist; a great artist steals." All top designers design alike, and we know great design when we see it. As soon as we walk into the room, the flowers are either graphic and accessible or they aren't. We'll immediately give a thumbs up or a thumbs down. And we'll usually be in agreement, like the four out of five dentists and the sugarless gum. This book will teach "the looks," and by the end of it you'll be hard-pressed to see top design on television shows and in magazines and not be able to figure out how to recreate that look.

This is a business, and you can be the greatest designer in the world and still be broke if you don't have a head for business. Plenty of mediocre designers are wildly successful simply because they're better at math, and can stay on top of their books. Cultivate relationships with clients and wholesalers, because you will only be able to get so far on design alone. Strive to be the most memorable, the most cheerful, and the most confident. Smile—that's Business 101!

Choose your business name very carefully. You want something you'll be happy with for decades to come. When I opened my first shop, I chose a terrible name. The building

Build a database of gorgeous flowers in the back of your brain, and before you know it, those looks will be readily available at your fingertips.

was an actual spinning windmill, which I thought was very Dutch and cute. Well, the name "Michael's" was already taken by a craft store, so I thought I'd get clever. I named my shop "Tulip-o-Mania," which was a period in Dutch history when tulip bulbs were traded like currency and were highly valued (it was between 1642 and 1646, and a single bulb sold for roughly $50,000 at today's prices. One day a botanist discovered that the most popular, ruffled strain of tulip was caused by a virus and wouldn't reproduce. Suddenly they were worthless, and the entire Dutch

economy collapsed. It's a true story; I hear Spielberg bought the rights to the book). Everyone who called the shop or came in asked, "You only sell tulips, right?" And I'd have to explain that we were a full-service shop. People passed me by thinking I was just nuts about tulips and didn't do anything else. It's difficult to change a name once you've established your business, so be sure to pick something you can live with for a long time and don't have to spell out or explain constantly. Many florists suddenly become French when naming their shops, and they're lovely names, but they're difficult to remember and to spell, and they might be off-putting to clients on a strict budget.

Make up business cards and hand them out to everyone who will stand still long enough to take one. Promote yourself! I started the first school in Milwaukee with a logo I drew with colored pencils at my kitchen counter. And then, instead of waiting for people to find out about it, I called an editor at the *Milwaukee Journal* and told her I had opened a flower design school. She said, "Wait, who are you?" And then she showed up twenty minutes later with reporters and a photographer to cover the school.

Flower designing can be done by anyone. I have yet to meet anyone that I cannot teach to produce gorgeous work. All design that you

come across in books and magazines can be broken down into a few simple formulae. If you understand those formulae, you can produce great floral design. I call myself the accidental florist. I stumbled on this trade and learned to love it. It's a great and honorable profession; florists are in the business of making people happy and helping them celebrate the important milestones in life.

Learn to think of yourself as a designer. I've had women come into my shop before and tell me they're planning on getting flowers wholesale and doing their own wedding, and I immediately talk them out of it. "I could teach you how to do it, but you won't be able to simply buy flowers off the street and make them look like they do in the magazines." Even if I did teach them, I promise them they don't want to be working that hard on their wedding day, and I get

"Flower designing can be done by anyone. I have yet to meet anyone that I cannot teach to produce gorgeous work."

them to book me. If tulips are selling at the grocery store down the street for $5 a bunch, you can't compete by selling that same bunch for $15. You will design it in a way that the grocery stores can't, and that the client buying them and taking them home can't either.

Make success happen for you. Think like a designer, walk and talk and act like a designer. I am a firm believer in the power of purposeful thinking. Call your local morning television show and offer yourself up as a guest for a segment. Come up with an angle that they might like— flowers for dogs or how to salvage an ugly mixed bouquet. There are flowers on the sets of soap operas. Call and find out how those can be

your flowers on the set. Take action, approach people fearlessly, and your business will bloom! Learn to develop a star quality. There are countless designers in the world—the ones that are truly successful are design stars.

This is your craft. The aim of this book is to teach you the craft. People will come to you for flowers because your designs are simply that much prettier, fresher, and higher quality than they've seen before. They will appreciate the two dozen tulips collared with variegated pittosporum more than the same vase with the same tulips that the other guys down the street simply plunked down into a vase, with the tulips flopping over the sides. They will see your skill in the slightest, smallest design. You are like

the couture designer, knowing when to add a button here and a seam there. You are like a chef who knows just the pinch of tarragon a dish needs to really shine. You will add that perfect touch of fiddlehead fern that makes the design uniquely yours. Clients will come to you because your work emotes feelings of beauty and love, and makes them feel at peace with the world for a few moments when they gaze at it.

MICHAEL GAFFNEY

MICHAEL GAFFNEY began his career on Wall Street before entering the floral industry. He teaches great design, as well as the economics, marketing, and philosophy behind a successful career in flowers. He has appeared on numerous television shows, and has designed for many films, weddings, and special events across the country. He calls many cities home, and in his spare time is usually found in the barn with his beloved thoroughbred horses.

KEITH LEWIS

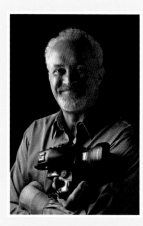

KEITH LEWIS has studied and practiced photography in the San Francisco Bay Area for many years. His business (www.avideye.com) serves a diverse clientele, from commercial enterprises to private customers, and his works have been displayed in solo and group exhibitions throughout the Bay Area. Keith is based in Berkeley, California, but his photography has appeared in three nationally published books: In the *Company of Flowers, A Glass Act,* and *A Celebration of Clematis.*

MATTHEW BUSHEY

MATTHEW BUSHEY is a fashion and beauty-based photographer whose work regularly appears in magazines and advertisements. His love for flowers and beautiful interiors immediately drew him to Michael and this book project, where he was excited to marry Michael's amazing design work to the beautiful spaces captured in these photos. Matthew also regularly creates limited print series of flower art. More of his work can be seen at his website, www.matthewbushey.com.